PEACE AND WAR

Nigel Mellor

Dab Hand Press

PEACE AND WAR

Copyright © Nigel Mellor 2017
All rights reserved

First published 2017 by
Dab Hand Press
Newcastle upon Tyne
http://sites.google.com/site/dabhandpress/

ISBN: 9780951386262

Designed by Ellen for Dab Hand Press

For Kate and Joe

Acknowledgements

Go forth and modify *Militant Thistles* (2017 forthcoming)
Sergeant Bill *The Great British Write Off*, Forward Poetry (2016)
Iraq, Libya, Syria, Brexit... *Culture Matters* **http://bit.ly/2lRp8d2_** (2016)
Beware of words *Simona Wallace plus 470 others* http://bit.ly/2jVXLNE (2015)
A small town on the river; Private Health Providers; Beware of words; How the West was lost; Austerity *Militant Thistles* http://bit.ly/2jABu7g (2013)
It starts with the libraries; Crisis management *The Robin Hood Book*, Caparison (2012)
Sergeant Bill; Negativity *Voices from the North East* Radio broadcast on NE1fm (June 22 2012)
The great Sainsbury's petrol station massacre of June 2026; Economics; Trickle down; Transformation; Go forth and modify *Emergency Verse*, Caparison (2011)
A modern cook book *The North East Poetry Journal* (2011)
A Johannesburg farmer discusses resistance, 1973 *Poetry Marathon*, Brian John Allen (1993)
Heroes *Guardians of The State*, Poetry Now (1992)

With thanks to: Carol, Fleur, Fran, Ginge, Joe and Carlotta, Kate and Adrian and Jack, Keith, Mark, Mary, Peter, Rosemary, Shaun and Molly, Yvonne.

Many of these poems may be best appreciated when read aloud.
To get a feel for the rhythm and accent of North East speech visit **http://bit.ly/Jazzcafepoetry**

Other Publications

Poetry

For the Inquiry: poetry of the dirty war. Dab Hand Press.

Buddhism

Buddhism#now: Big Questions. Inner Peace. LOL. Dab Hand Press.

Practitioner books

Attention Seeking: a complete guide for teachers. Sage.
The Good, the Bad and the Irritating: A practical approach for parents of children who are attention seeking. Sage.

Contents

PEACE

1. ENVIRONMENT AND IMPERMANENCE

- 17 The great Sainsbury's petrol station massacre of June 2026
- 18 Settle
- 20 The gateway: at the confluence of the North and South Tyne
- 21 Windermere
- 22 The appearance and disappearance of birds
- 23 In an easterly light
- 24 The rescue
- 25 Incident in the fishing grounds
- 26 Gene story
- 27 At the rising of the seas
- 28 The noble sacrifice of whales
- 29 If you'd just told me
- 30 We all hate flies
- 31 Go forth and modify
- 32 Return
- 33 The walk
- 34 Chapter and verse

2. TO INDIA WITH LOVE

- 37 Mumbai, late
- 38 We didn't want the Taj hotel
- 39 Big city
- 40 Village
- 41 Near Osho International Meditation Resort

42 Gin and Tonic at the Residency Club, Pune
43 Jai Hind
3. RELATIONSHIPS
47 The rosewood casket
48 1950s
49 The point
50 Control freak
51 Model
52 The sand wiggler
53 Before getting in
54 The Cluny, Ouseburn Valley
55 By Constant Rise
56 Dreams of Polly Toynbee
57 That man
58 Chains
59 Christmas
60 Negativity
61 Right On
62 On the naïve belief in the transformative power of pop records
63 Semi on the Coast Road, 1973
64 These matter
65 On silence
4. ON MORTALITY AND RELIGION
69 Nursing Home, 1991
71 The hawk moth
72 The tin plate from the Victorian mine
73 August 1999 – an earthquake in Turkey
74 Appellation Contrôlée, wine label 'Minervois'
75 Getting older

76 An excess of miracles
77 On medievalism
78 I believe
79 Say a silent prayer
80 Seaton Delaval hall
81 Why did Di die?
82 Toddler Alan Kurdi, 2015
83 After visiting hours, 2014
84 A church service
85 Funeral gathering
86 In passing
87 Gods

5. ECONOMICS AND POLITICS

91 Heroes
92 Memo to the informer, now
93 Human Rights
94 A Johannesburg farmer discusses resistance, 1973
95 Beware of words
96 A reflection on the irony surrounding the long delayed trial of the Right Honourable Anthony Charles Lynton Blair at the International Criminal Court
97 Iraq Libya Syria Brexit....
98 A modern cook book
99 Songs of praise (for a guy)
100 The peculiar similarities of 1939 and 2017
101 Nation state
102 Reason
103 The way

104	How the West was lost
105	Trickle down
106	Destitution
107	Austerity
108	Private Health Providers
109	What I find annoying on reading autobiographies of Important People
110	It starts with the libraries
111	Transformation
112	Crisis management
113	Economics
114	Mr. President-for-life
115	Lessons

AND

119	Becoming

WAR

123	The tile maker of Darnac
124	A letter to the recruiting sergeant
125	Edith Cavell, October 12 1915, dawn
126	This and that
127	Poppy Day
128	I seem to see
129	The final Samurai battle
130	When war comes
131	Long, long ago
132	Peace
133	Philosophy for soldiers, level 1
134	Leftie
135	Civil War
136	An old woman climbs Starshaw Bank

- 137 The mother's tale
- 138 Stand up
- 139 The cornflake man
- 140 Control
- 141 Libya: mission creep
- 142 Saddam
- 143 A small town on the river
- 144 Revenge
- 145 Holiday in Andalucia, Spring 2011
- 146 Sergeant Bill
- 148 Nigel Mellor's Reviews

PEACE

Peace is rarely peaceful

1. ENVIRONMENT AND IMPERMANENCE

The great Sainsbury's petrol station massacre of June 2026

> There is no more terrifying sight
> Than the middle classes
> Short on
> Fuel

Settle

The ringing drew me

I'm certain I hadn't heard a blacksmith working since I was a child, and can't really recall one then, living in the town, not the country, as we did

But the ringing drew me

That special sound of the beating on the anvil while waiting the next beat on the metal, to keep the rhythm going

You see, the ringing drew me

We got return tickets on the Carlisle to Settle line, but couldn't get steam. And the viaduct is not so impressive from the train window (you have to get out and walk back, which we didn't)

Which is just as well, because the ringing drew me

We poked round antique shops and picked up some curd cheesecake, which we'd been looking for, for years since we found a monastery on the moors and bought a cheesecake, and loved it. Then lost it for ever. The monastery, that is

And all the time the ringing drew me

Even when we climbed the crag and watched the quarry lorries almost meeting on the tightest turn – the up-wagons slow and dragging, the down-wagons fast and bouncing – on the busiest road through what should have been calm

The ringing drew me

The smith was happy to stop and chat, and we took photos, and a business card. Not that we intended to have fancy wrought iron railings made, but we wanted to look as though we just might. In thanks

As I remember it, it was the ringing that drew me

To a past I never knew I knew

The gateway: at the confluence of the North and South Tyne

Where peat-brown water off the border
Rages down
On the soft, sweet stream from the south
At that mingling
I knew the Roman who stopped to drink his fill
And all the ghosts to come.

Windermere

Leaving
On the quarter to four
The forward motion of the boat
Exactly balanced the wind

The bow flag stilled
And with engines on half-ahead
All was hushed
As the ferry slid
Into a time gone by

The appearance and disappearance of birds

The death of her mate
Upset the swan watcher
Not the swan
    -o-
The seagulls' cries
Of drowned sailors, by day
Become the silent shades of night
    -o-
And my kestrel has gone
From the field
Where the new B&Q superstore lies
    -o-
But I know the branch
Where the kingfisher sits
On those rare occasions
When he crosses my route.
I am blessed
I can say no less.
And I can say no more.

In an easterly light

About nine tenths of the way
By my reckoning
At the very limit of my eye's reach
A speck twisted
Now with sails, now without

But the harder I strained
The harder it was
To pick out that struggling
Between sky
And the waiting sea

The rescue

We could not stare
At the rescue
And we could give no help

If the worst that could happen
Did happen
As we watched
Would we have felt unclean?

Incident in the fishing grounds

Cromarty Forth Tyne
Severe gales increasing to hurricane force twelve
Imminent

The cabin light
Was twenty feet off

He was wet beneath the oilskin
His hands were numb

He did not see
The wave from behind

Cromarty Forth Tyne
Severe gales increasing to hurricane force twelve
Imminent

Gene story*

I am the last of my kind
Chipping on rock:
"Once were humans"

it is now possible for backyard chemists to switch genes around, with no regulation

At the rising of the seas*

Warnings came and warnings went
You still wanted everything

But when we lost Manhattan
They even listened in Beijing

with apologies to Leonard Cohen

The noble sacrifice of whales

With no way to cry "stop"
They came, silent
To die on our beaches

If you'd just told me

Look, the oceans are finished
The land is gone
The air isn't fit to breathe

If you'd just told me

Of course I would have done anything
I would've stopped driving
Or flying
Or … something

I just didn't know

You can't blame me
What was I supposed to do?

If you'd just told me

We all hate flies*

No one worried
When the flies went

But quite soon after
We went too

for Silent Spring

Go forth and modify

Across all the lands
The new corn grew strong
Until the twentieth generation
When crops simply failed

Then we begged from the poorest
Seeds from the old days
Too precious to eat

Return

A century we thought them done

But now we're digging out pits
And building up the fires

What we tried to kill
We only made stronger

It is the plague times, again
It is the plague times

The walk

He walked for two weeks
Carrying his brother
They ate when they could
Mostly there was nothing

A child himself
All he had was the walk
His brother
And the rumour of a camp

Chapter and verse

And they shall have dominion over
every thing that walks and crawls
and slithers and slides
and swims and flies
and grows in tangles on the good earth.
And that dominion shall be as love

2. TO INDIA WITH LOVE

Mumbai, late

From darkness
So small and dusty
Holding hands through the traffic
They walked off
Into India

We didn't want the Taj hotel

Just a few yards along the shore
The carpet was threadbare
And the sheets needed mending
But when we opened the shutters
A warm wind blew in from the Arabian sea.
In that one movement
The country was ours

Big city

A water buffalo and her calf wading the river
Sheets drying on rocks
Cries from the circling kite hawks
And twenty four hour traffic on the bridge

Village

Shiva's temple by the haystack
Stone steps to the river
A sari of crimson and gold

An infant in the sunset
And a dog left dying on the road

Near Osho International Meditation Resort

Holy Western guru
Saintly face
Loving the poor fruit seller
Buying nothing

Gin and Tonic at the Residency Club, Pune

As we signed the photo
"Gina and Tonic at the Residency Club, Pune"
(a gentle joke for friends)
We became my parents
Under the Raj

But then the image changed again
To a picture in a scrapbook
Discovered by grandchildren
Yet unborn

Jai Hind

We are the children
Of the lost Empire
When we go
It goes too

It is not the fashion these days
Nor is it politically correct
To talk of

Leaving Simla on a mule
Sunrise over the Taj Mahal
A glimpse of the Himalayas
Dinner under the moon
And the infant who died in the heat of the South

All that is left
Is to whisper at Ghandi's tomb
Jai Hind – long live India

3. RELATIONSHIPS

The rosewood casket

I like the metric system
It's sensible
It works
It's plain as plain can be

But for that rosewood casket
Hand carved with feeling
Inches and eighths
Were the language of love

1950s

I recall
In a lane
Two boys with sticks
Whacking an ancient hedge
Which hurt neither hedge
Nor boys
    -o-
Empty, quiet streets
Cold breeze
Hot tar
Back from the park with wet feet
And Davey
    -o-
Tinned salmon
Cucumber, thinly sliced
Neat lettuce
Tomatoes with no taste
Talk at tea time.
And nothing ever said

The point

Why were you so awful?
Made me feel small,
Uncomfortable.

We could have been colleagues.
Dare I say it,
Friends?

Forty years on,
Now I can see
The dying in your face,
And the problems gone
(whatever they were),
What was the point?

Control freak

I did not know
There was a wrong way
To blow dandelion clocks

Model

what she really
really wanted was
someone to
walk beside her night
and day carrying
a full length
mirror

The sand wiggler

Under the beach umbrella
After too many margaritas
Than was strictly sensible at my age
I spied the sand wiggler

Over dunes and rocks he followed a random tack
Chasing food? Water? Sex?
I suppose he had a Latin name
But had not learned it

My glance was taken by a dancer
And children playing
Then he was gone

Returning to the hotel
From the furthest corner of my eye
I think I saw him, one last time
Going about his life
As I went about mine

Before getting in

This stretch of coast
Is particularly treacherous

They say
When the tide slips in on the surface
Quiet, sly
Strong currents drag
Whatever lies beneath
Up the bay
Then down
Sometimes, simply, out

It is important to know the sea
Before getting into the water

The Cluny, Ouseburn Valley

There is a grassy bank outside my pub
Although it's not properly a pub
More a "venue"
And the bank is pretty boring

But the glass you look through isn't

The windows are old
Very old
And some panes remain
From the day

Watching him
Coming down the bank
Bent this way and that
By the faulted glass
I wondered what was real
Him
The bank
Or the glass?

By Constant Rise

I watched you as you climbed that hill
Now clear
Now hidden by a bush
Now a turn in the path

I watched you long after you had gone
Even when the way itself could not be seen

I watched you till the stars gave out
And the birds brought back the day

I watched you till my eyes hurt
And my body grew so very, very cold

I watched you
Because the watching was all I had

Dreams of Polly Toynbee

On my bus-pass-birthday trip
To Eastern Europe
She kept to herself

With a smoky laugh
And quick temper
She liked a drink
And was the spit

But at the border
Needed to complain
That Birmingham, with all the robes
(she meant the races)
No longer looked like England

So, gone my dream of Polly Toynbee
And gone my chance of fame

That man

Mark that man
Plot his course
On maps and measure well
Chart his destination

Take down every syllable
And carefully note
Each gesture, hint or finger raised

Don't let one breath
Of that man's passage
Escape your close attention

Because that man lies

His words are screens
You may forget

Then he will act

Chains

My walls are open fields
My chains are winding roads

How can I go to my love
When I do not know if my love loves me

My father would ask, my brothers would mock

If it were market day, we'd be there by dawn
If it were wedding day, we'd be there by noon
But to go without reason
To go without knowing
Just to go!

The village has no locks
My walls are open fields
My chains are winding roads

Christmas

I had forgotten
So much

But that tree
In the back of the old Volvo
Had the scent

I drove home
Disturbed

Negativity

I am really not bothered what you think
And although your words depress me
They will not stop me

Because all my life
I have seen distant hills

Right on

He had dealt
amazingly successfully
with sexism racism
classism ageism
and even able-bodied-ism
but at the end of the day
he was still
a total
shit

On the naïve belief in the transformative power of pop records

We were so young

With all that music
We thought we could
Change the world

We couldn't even
Change ourselves

Semi on the Coast Road, 1973

Old fashioned Sunday
Cuddled in the fire glow
Mary and her cat

Listening to the sound of radios and rain
Listening to the sounds
Listening to the sound of night cars hissing by

These matter

After all I've done
And all I've been
Only these remain

A hand in mine
A track to nowhere on an endless day
A blackberry bush

And her silly joke

On silence

There is the quiet
Of an empty house
Then there is the empty quiet
When the children have gone

4. ON MORTALITY AND RELIGION

Nursing Home, 1991

Try a drop of tea, Pa. I've
Put a bit of sugar
In, I know I shouldn't. They
Brought me a full pot on
A tray with two rows
Of biscuits on a plate in
Circles and a glass
Of sherry. Hope it's not
South African
-o-
No, I'm the younger one, my brother's
The older one with
A beard. At least I think he's
Got a beard. It's funny, I see him every
Day and I can't remember

Yes it has turned
Cold in here. I didn't notice you
Opened the window. I covered him
Up, he seemed cold
-o-
They're coming to turn
You in a minute, Pa, they
Like me to leave then, I
Get in the way and they need
To wash you
-o-

They call him Bill and
Talk to him while they do
Their job and now they've asked that
Young nurse to look after
Someone in the next room – he's
Been coughing again and
Through the night I can hear them talking gently
To the others as
They put them to bed, and it's
Not put on for my benefit
    -o-
I wonder where the rest of your
Cups and medals are. Ma brought them
In with a picture of your dad and
The children were pleased to come
Today although we all just sat
And cried, but they weren't too young to
Understand that moving
To the hospital with tubes and drips
Wasn't right. They
Said you wouldn't want that
    -o-
Can you hear me
Pa? It's me. Hold
My hand. I love you. And
Thanks.

The hawk moth

Beating itself against the window
The hawk moth
Despite my fond desire
Could not live
But would not die

The tin plate from the Victorian mine

Mines used to be so much simpler

There was one way in
And one way out

But when the tunnel collapsed
There was no way out

Months later
The recovery team found
Beside the bodies
Scratched on a tin plate
"I don't want to die in the dark"

August 1999 – an earthquake in Turkey

My sister was called Tasneem
She was named after the fountain in the garden of
Paradise

I remember the shaking most

The man who used to live in the other room
Cried a lot
He died the first day
I knew it was day because the blackness was not quite so
black

We shouted
But could hardly make a sound
The second day

I think I heard her cry, when the bulldozers came
There was so much noise

My sister was named after the fountain in the garden of
Paradise

Appellation Contrôlée, wine label 'Minervois'

Under a warm sea
The shells of dying creatures
Laid down the soil
Of Minervois

It is recorded that

In the year of our Lord
Twelve hundred and ten
Men, women and children
Of a peaceful faith
Threw themselves on the fires
Of Simon de Montfort

Now
They kiss cheeks
In greeting
And the land is still

Getting older

My enthusiastic
friend
said give it
a go, you'll regret
it if you don't
so I did and I
enjoyed it
now I've done it
and I'm still not
famous
I wonder whether being
left with
my illusions
would have been
the kinder thing

An excess of miracles

I'm bored with miracles

What I mean is
The first one was, well, miraculous
And the second
Right up to about number eighty three
But then it started to get a bit
Repetitive

Don't get me wrong
It's wonderful and all that
But you can't spend your day
Just marvelling

Life has to go on
Miracles or no

On medievalism

There must be
One hundred books on gods
And one hundred books on goddesses
One hundred books on devils
And one hundred books on angels
One hundred books on wizards
And one hundred books on witches
One hundred books on heaven
And one hundred books on hell
One hundred books on cherubs
And one hundred books on demons
One hundred books on telepathy
And one hundred books on levitation
One hundred books on astrology
And one hundred books on reincarnation
One hundred books on miracles
And one hundred books on spells
And they can all simply be
Wrong

I believe*

I believe
Beliefs bereave
Bedevil. Besmirch.
Betwixt. Between.

Be without end.
Be upstanding.
Bewitch Bother and Bewilder.
Be grateful for.

Be gone Beelzebub and all his works.
Be still, the voice of calm.
Beware.
Be everywhere.

Be mine.
Be thine.
Be on time.
Be the best you can.

And
Be a man my son.

from a workshop on "be"

Say a silent prayer

I prayed the bus wouldn't be late
But maybe I should have
Prayed I hadn't lost the tickets
But maybe I should have
Prayed he would get his job
But maybe I should have
Prayed the baby would get well
But maybe I should have
Prayed they caught the bomber quickly
But maybe I should have
Prayed the ice caps wouldn't melt
But maybe I should have
Prayed the meteor couldn't get us
But maybe I should have
Given up on prayer

Seaton Delaval hall

From Laval in France
They conquered with William
The wild Delavals
Had competitions in grinning
And biting the heads off sparrows

Now children run in their empty halls
How the flighty are fallen

Why did Di die?

I didn't spy
With my little eye
Or cause her to fly

I didn't buy
The journals that pry
(and pay the paparazzi guy
 to take pix from the sky)

I didn't sigh
Or identify
Or drool over lie
After lie after lie after lie

And I know you'll deny
(as you openly try
to deify Di,
while all on the sly
you'd read how she'd cry)
It was you made her die

Toddler Alan Kurdi, 2015

He lay there
To open our hearts
And sleep forever on a foreign shore

After visiting hours, 2014

Towards the end
There are promises
That will not be kept
Remembrances taken away
And one last skill to learn:
To drive and cry

A church service

The only important mystery
Is life
From font to tomb

The times before and beyond
The mouldering church knows well
But wisely remains silent

Funeral gathering

We think we are
The centre of the universe
But what it comes down to
Is scraps of people
Tears
Sandwiches
And a nice cup of tea

In passing

You can measure a life
In plastic bags

Ornaments
That aren't worth much
Clothes that no one wants
Photos that might mean something
To somebody
A battered brass pot
From the mystic East

Soon the memories will go too
Out with the bags

Gods

Children need adults
The way adults need gods,
To take away the pain
And answer the question

There are, however,
Only children and adults

5. ECONOMICS AND POLITICS

Heroes*

There are no guarantees

It's great at the end
When the heroes come out
And everything's put to rights

But what about the start?

You're like me, my friend
I waited twenty years
Till it was safe to be brave

following a revolution in Eastern Europe

Memo to the informer, now*

When we are old
And you want my forgiveness
And you try to explain the pressures you were under
I might listen

But, then again, I might not

* after revelations of extensive secret files in Germany and Poland

Human Rights

When the bombs go off
The gloves come off
Then the only thing we have to stand up for
We throw out in the uproar

Justice is top prize in the dirty war

A Johannesburg farmer discusses resistance, 1973

In my head it was right
In my heart it was right
But I did not know it was right
Until I heard the soft warm voice of Africa

Beware of words

To kill them
You must first
Make them less than human

And all that takes
Is words

A reflection on the irony surrounding the long delayed trial of the Right Honourable Anthony Charles Lynton Blair at the International Criminal Court

The one time
He told the truth
The whole truth
And nothing but the truth
Nobody believed him

Iraq Libya Syria Brexit....

Bring up, bring up the guilty men
Who fooled us all along
Without a plan if things went right
Or a plan if things went wrong

A modern cook book

Starters

Take one dictator
Arm to the hilt
Suppress the news
And all opposition
Sprinkle with spies
And secret police
Leave in a dark space to ferment
Then complain about the mess

Main course

Take one nuclear reactor
Place on active fault line
Give a bit of a shake
Rely on hose pipes
When the cooling system fails
Call on the state to clean up the mess
Thank heaven that no one dies
Then announce "nuclear power is safe"

Dessert

Take one Tory government

No, stop! I feel sick

Songs of praise (for a guy)

Obama
O charmer
Osama (not)

O dreamer
O schemer
O George Bush (not)

O walker
O talker
O Gordon Brown (not)

O leader
O pleader
O Cameron (not)

O Dancer
O Prancer
O Santa Claus (not)

And you can't help liking him
Even if he is American

The peculiar similarities of 1939 and 2017

It feels strangely like

The unsettled peace before
THE BIG ONE
Before
THE BALLOON WENT UP
Before
ALL HELL BROKE LOOSE

The difference is
We know we survived that time

Nation state

It takes a lifetime to build a nation
Sadly
It also takes many lives

Reason

There is always a good reason for

Detention
Closing newspapers
Secret trials
Assassination
And the pulling out of fingernails

The thing is
Never
Accept
The reason

The way

'tis the way of the rebel
to cast off the iron chains
of oppression
only
to slip into the shiny plastic suit
of commerce
which grips
just as tight

How the West was lost

When politicians cheat and bankers lie
And newspapers won't fight the good fight
The man in the street joins the army's old cry
For a strong man to put it all right

Trickle down

The spectacularly fraudulent trick
Behind the theory of trickle down
Is that money is actually persuaded to flow
Uphill
From poor to rich
Not t'other way round

Destitution

The road from welfare
To workhouse
Is very short
And it goes via shame

Austerity

There will come a day
When you will work
Not for wages
But just the bread to fill your belly

And on that day
Banks will, as usual,
Fail disastrously
And ask you to eat less bread

Private Health Providers

First they came for the glasses
And I said nothing because I could afford glasses

Then they came for the teeth
And I said nothing because I could afford teeth

Then they came for the warts
And I said nothing because I could afford warts

Then they came for the heart surgery

What I find annoying on reading autobiographies of Important People

It's not that
They had money
And connections
And servants

It's that
We didn't have
Money
Or connections

And we were the servants

It starts with the libraries

Few of the gentle
Little things
Survive the crushing wheel
To market
Which is, perhaps, the point

When the flowers have gone
Can the oaks be far behind?

Transformation

The only way to make the poor richer
Is to make the poor richer
Making the rich richer never works

Crisis management

When bankers riot
And investors pull down the City of London
We calm them with trillions

When youths riot
And children pull down the inner city
We calm them with truncheons

Economics

Imagine the impact
On the dismal science of economics
If, in standard text books,
Whenever we saw the words "the markets"
We substituted the, admittedly rather cumbersome, phrase
"a small collection of highly paid men"

Mr. President-for-life

Rule by fear
Can be remarkably successful

I know that
And so do you

But there is one tiny, weak link
In this whole enterprise

Fear can leave
Then so must you

Lessons

Fascism does not come
With horns on the head
Cloven hooves
And a tail

No

It comes with smiles
And votes
And hatred in the heart

AND

A few friends, in strictest anonymity, have alluded to what bubbles up beneath.

Becoming

You are tough
I can see it in the way you look
In your voice
You are the kind I cannot hurt
My words have no effect
Neither have my deeds

But you
You hurt me
You can break me with ease
And you have done
Many times

But I have survived
I have learned
Slowly
Each time a little more

Now I am steel
Broken, but re-forged

You have not yet been tested

WAR

We can be proud of that golden generation who served. Pa loved the army, but war is another matter; and, perhaps unsurprisingly, women's voices are often missing. Some of the following pieces attempt to correct this.

The tile maker of Darnac

I came to know this man
The tile maker of Darnac
As we moved one hundred hundred
Of his curved French tiles
To roof the old barn

A tall man, I sensed,
The clay shaped over his thigh
Tapering to the knee
Trimmed and fired red
To last through time

A few shorter and finer
Perhaps his partner's
All strong yet easily broken
But no matter how small the overlap
They cling to protect the layer beneath

Are their names now
In the pilgrim's church
With the fallen of the Great War?
Listed, not as soldiers,
But as "children of this parish"

A letter to the recruiting sergeant

From the way you talk
He could have been stamped out in a factory

But he's mine

Eighteen years of work
That's six thousand five hundred
And seventy days, to you, mister

And you're not 'avin' 'im

Edith Cavell, October 12 1915, dawn

I don't care
What you call them
Or what uniforms they wear
To me they are just men
In pain
Though some are hardly grown

Perhaps they will fight again
That's not my decision

I am a nurse, nobody's saint
Not afraid of death
I have known so much
Just let me see the sun one more time

Then shoot

This and that

People on this side
People on that
All found the same ways of dying

Some did it quick
Some did it clean
And some did it slow while crying

Poppy Day

We remember the soldier with a gun
Who is such a brave fighter

Not the mother with a child
Who can only hold tighter

I seem to see

I seem to see
Through the long strands of mind

A war
Not my father's
(which ended just as I
was getting going)
But the one before
With greatcoats
And gas

A park
With railings and wardens

Dark, heavy rooms and
A woman
In a long costume

Not paintings
Not engravings
No
I see through memories

The final Samurai battle

Drawing their swords
They ran at the guns

It is said that the soldiers cried
As they shot them down

When war comes

When war comes
(and it will)
Those you now despise
(the unemployed, the riff-raff)
Will become your legends

All it needs is war

Long, long ago

Things were much slower then

It took ten thousand men in one army
To slaughter ten thousand men in the other
And the whole bloody business took days

Peace

It is sad but true
For peace to reign
Finally
The weak must forgive the strong
And the wronged, the wrong doer

Philosophy for soldiers, level 1

Re-sit, September.

You have one question.
Time 45 minutes.
Please use both sides of the paper.

In a crisis
Economic or otherwise
Should you
A. Shoot unarmed civilians
B. Desert

DISCUSS

Leftie

I'm a leftie
And a pacifist
And to be quite honest
A bit of a wimp

To me the average squaddie
Is, well…

But when push comes to shove
You know who's got your back

Civil War

The tighter the ties that bind
The deeper the cuts when torn

An old woman climbs Starshaw Bank

Thank you kind sir
But I'll carry my own bag
Up Starshaw Bank

My father fell in the Great War
My husband died in Normandy, I kept his medal
My lad, it was the Falklands
They say he had courage

You see, I'm a real army wife

And each day I must carry my own bag
Up Starshaw Bank

The mother's tale

He will always be a hero to me
My son
Although we don't talk about
Such things these days

I found out how he died
The exact time and place
I've even met the regiment that did him in

But I don't hate them
They're friends now
The British

Stand up*

"It couldn't happen here"
You say

"We wouldn't let it"
You say

But you don't even open your mouth in staff meetings

You don't say

for the anniversary of the liberation of Auschwitz

The cornflake man*

Lenny was a poor shot
So they gave him a flame thrower

We had the heavy machine gun
As we went through towns and villages

I don't like to think about those times

Now I am in the factory
I make your cornflakes

I am the cornflake man

for much older friends, 1939-45

Control *

sometimes they left
their radios
on, those poor
boys we heard
them as they
went
down
screaming

for the anniversary of the Battle of Britain

Libya: mission creep

look out for
that subtle point
when "Just War"
becomes
just war

Saddam

We rejoice
Over the death of one man
But before we declare the world
A safer place
We should be sure
That we know the nature of
The man
The world
And the meaning of the word 'safer'

A small town on the river

Tonight the beer is dark
I don't understand why

The barges are low in the water
Waves wash along the decks

I share a word of pleasure with a stranger,
In her language,
As we watch a heron pose

The accordion player smiles right into my eyes
In thanks for a coin

In the crowd the football songs are the same

Students, well drunken
Ask the way to the old town
And apologize for their schoolboy English

Over fish soup
Two businessmen write down where to visit,
Discuss the war
And Clint Eastwood, who they'd met on holiday

Why should anyone want to kill these people?

Revenge

Revenge
Is understandable
(and can we disagree?)
But what gives hope
Is the woman whose husband
Never came home
Yet can say
The killing
Stops
With
Me

Holiday in Andalucia, Spring 2011

In the small towns of Southern Spain
Drivers stop
To let you cross the road

We choose to eat
Spaghetti Bolognese
On the beach

The air is fragrant
Orange trees
Have both oranges and blossom
At the same time

You can see the coast of Africa

When the wind drops
The sand is too hot for bare feet

And not too far away
Across the ancient Mediterranean
Men are trying to blow each other to pieces
And families are drowning to be free

Sergeant Bill

Where are you lying now, my sergeant Bill?
They sent me back your letters, sergeant Bill
Sent me caps and sent a kitbag
Sent me boxes and a bold flag
But no one thought to send me sergeant Bill

Shipped you off like cargo, sergeant Bill
Stamped and documented, sergeant Bill
Gave you boots and gave you Blanco
An old rifle and some ammo
But no quartermaster gave me sergeant Bill

Where are you lying now, my sergeant Bill?
Telegrams forgot to say, my sergeant Bill
Said how proud they were and grateful
Great deeds you did, but fatal
But paper's not the same as sergeant Bill

I suppose you did your duty, sergeant Bill
Still I'd rather have a coward, sergeant Bill
To hold me and to need me
To love me and to feed me
Through all the years you leave me, sergeant Bill

If you enjoyed this book the author would welcome a review. These can be posted on Amazon or any site where you downloaded an ebook.

Nigel Mellor's Reviews

Reviews of **For the Inquiry: Poetry of the dirty war.** *(Dab Hand Press)*

An excellent collection. ***Tribune***
There is a special ring to Mellor's poetry. It's a unique compelling, boiled-down style which manages to convey a deep sense of cultural unease that many will surely recognise . . . a collection to establish his work among the first rank. ***7 Days***
Honest, straight talking . . . political in the best sense . . . keeps the human perspective firmly in view . . . A timely reminder that poetry has an important role . . . Should be read by all who share the author's fear that 'the freedoms we have . . . become a way of forgetting. ***Carol Rumens***
If the Inquiry is no charade, it will take these words to heart. As will the reader . . . A plain man's guide to political breakdown . . . This is caring unsentimental poetry. ***Gillian Allnutt***
Mellor has a clean, sparse ... engaging style. For the Inquiry... is a beguiling collection, its poems ... deceptively simple ... their subversive nursery-rhyme style charm cradled over deeper wells of meaning, even occasionally, of the sublime. ***Alan Morrison***

Available on Amazon and www.nmellor.com

 Reviews of **Buddhism#now: Big Questions. Inner Peace. LOL.** *(Dab Hand Press)*

Dr. Mellor really knows his stuff ... entertaining ...unique and amusing ... brilliantly diverse coverage ... thoroughly enjoyable. ***The Courier***
This world needs more authors like Nigel Mellor. He brings such light and explanation to serious questions. ***Amazon***
A good read ... combines slapstick humour with everyday life experiences ... without jargon or mysticism. ***NSU/Life***
With this gem of a book Nigel Mellor has delivered something that is simultaneously light and funny and packed with sincerity and wisdom. ***Amazon***
Crystal clear jokey writing, cartoons and snappy dialogue. ***Engage***
Fantastic, funny, insightful read. ***Amazon***
Informative ... find the distinction between pleasure and long-lasting happiness ... readable. ***Lifestyle***
A beautiful book ... for serious thinkers and for people who want to know the secrets and meanings of life. ***Amazon***
Fresh, original, captivating and insightful. ***Amazon***

 Reviews of **The good, the bad and the irritating: A practical approach for parents of children who are attention seeking.** *(Sage)*

Over 20 years Dr Mellor has developed strategies that ... effectively change the child's behaviour. **The Independent**
Full of hope ... for parents [in] a desperate world. Advice is given with understanding, warmth and a real appreciation of what life is like when you have an impossible child. **Times Educational Supplement**
A very practical, down-to-earth and humorous approach... techniques that harassed parents can use ... this book is impressive. **Educational Psychology in Practice**
Extremely useful... I recommend this book as a manual for parenthood. Humour makes it an entertaining, yet informative read. **The Teacher**
Highly enjoyable ...delivers key messages superbly well... points are delivered with warmth and sensitivity. **British Journal of Special Education**
[Mellor's] techniques will help you to turn your child from a monster into an angel. **Daily Express**
Who's pulling the strings? ... strategies [for] exasperated parents. **Yorkshire Post**
They are driving parents mad ... but there is a consistent approach that helps. **Birmingham Post**

Back to your granny's wise words - the book is packed with real life examples ...[from] families and their moments of sheer desperation. **Sheffield Star**

The parents [Dr Mellor] sees are in a terrible state ... [his] help is practical and focused on the future rather than past mistakes. **Newcastle Journal**

I immediately felt a lot of empathy. All in all an excellent book. **Special**

Up-front and practical approach to this all-encompassing challenge. **Education and Health**

A very valuable resource. **Children are Unbeatable Alliance**

Empowers parents ....would be ideal at parent workshops. **Special Needs Information Press**

A panacea for many parents ... an immensely readable book. **Young Minds**

Mellor's easy-going and empathetic style of writing [is] both refreshing and eminently readable ... the book is shot through with humour, modesty and encouragement and I highly recommend it. **Contact a Family**

 Reviews of **Attention seeking: a complete guide for teachers**. *(Sage)*

Help is now at hand ... for the teachers ... driven to despair... gives teachers a way of gaining control. **Times Educational Supplement**
Practical strategies [to counter these] weapons of mass disruption. **The Guardian**
Even makes enjoyable bedtime reading, since Mellor's style is easy and interesting ... case studies ... bring the book alive. **Special Children**
Good, sound advice ... a valuable book for those involved in teacher-training. **Educational Psychology in Practice**
An abundance of common sense. **Education and Health**
For the harassed teacher ... invaluable. **Child Care Forum**
Advice... is well-founded and user-friendly. **Bridges, Northumbria University**
They drive adults up the wall... attention seeking children have so far struggled to find a category of their own in the experts' text-books. **Education Journal**
A pioneering book ... from a wealth of practical experience. **Herald and Post**

www.ingramcontent.com/pod-product-compliance
Lightning Source LLC
Chambersburg PA
CBHW060506030426
42337CB00015B/1769